IMAGES
of America

IRVINGTON

Alan A. Siegel

First published 1997

ISBN 0-7524-0589-6

Published by Arcadia Publishing,
an imprint of the Chalford Publishing Corporation
One Washington Center, Dover, New Hampshire 03820
Printed in Great Britain

Library of Congress Cataloging-in-Publication Data applied for

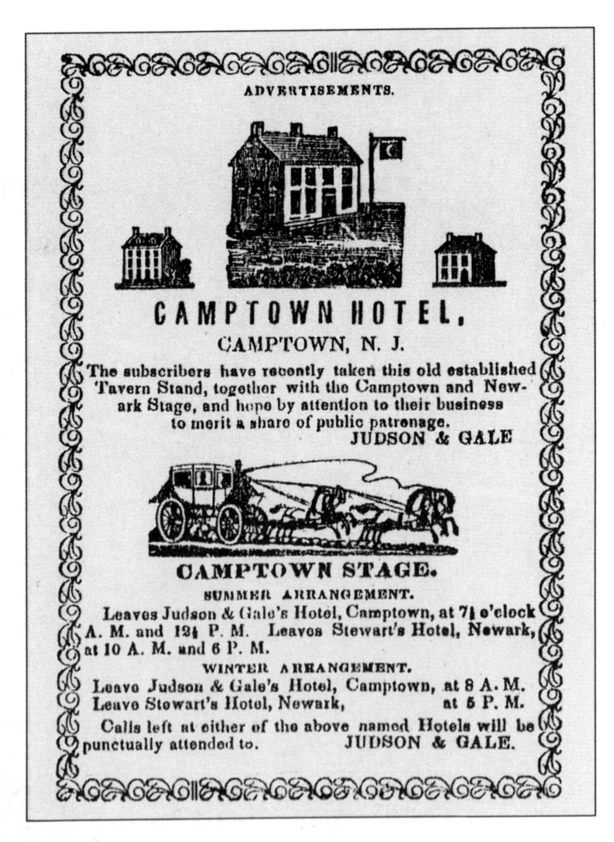

James P. Judson and William G. Gale's advertisement in *Pierson's City of Newark Directory*, 1847 edition.

Contents

Acknowledgments

The author expresses his thanks to all those who contributed photographs or information to this book, including: Loretta Gibbs and Harold Mann of the Irvington Tax Assessor's Office; Alma Simonitsch; Herbert Ramo; Christine McCloskey; C. Stewart Hausmann; Clifton C. Streeter; Wilma Perina; the staff at the New Jersey Room, Newark Public Library; President Harry Stevenson and members of the Irvington Historical Society for allowing me to use photos from the Society's collection; Lorelei McConnell and Roberta Rosen of the Irvington Public Library; and, last but certainly not least, those good folks at Arcadia Publishing who are doing such a commendable job preserving the images of our nation's past by publishing the best of them in their series of photographic histories.

Many of the photos in this book are from the collection of the Irvington Public Library, a treasure-trove of more than 1,100 photographs that in its scope and quality may well be one of the finest in New Jersey. Through the combined efforts of Library Director Lorelei McConnell and Assistant Director Roberta Rosen, the library has recently insured the preservation of these irreplaceable photos and their accessibility to the people of this state.

Thanks to the New Jersey Historical Commission, the Irvington Library obtained an evaluation of its collection by a professional conservator. Concerned and knowledgeable staff of libraries with similar collections gave freely of their experience. Finally, the New Jersey State Library funded Irvington's efforts through two successive annual Maintenance of Library Collections grants.

The original photographs are now safely stored under improved archival conditions. For the first time, negatives are available to produce additional copies as needed. Using the newest processes, each image has been transferred to microfilm, another archival medium. The original microfilm rolls are now stored in the vaults of the State Archives in Trenton with copies at the New Jersey State Library in Trenton, Rutgers Special Collections in New Brunswick, the New Jersey Historical Society, Newark, and the New Jersey Room, Newark Public Library. Descriptions of each image are recorded in a computer database which is similarly available. Readers who find this book of interest can learn much more about Irvington's past by visiting the Irvington Public Library on Civic Square or by consulting my earlier book, *Out of Our Past*, published in 1974.

Alan A. Siegel
May 20, 1997

A Brief History of Irvington

Fifteen thousand years ago what is now Irvington lay buried under hundreds of feet of glacial ice. As the climate gradually tempered, the glacier loosened its frigid grasp upon the land, and the present-day contours of the town emerged. The Elizabeth River is the chief geographic feature of Irvington, bisecting the town from north to south. The river, which enters Irvington at a point 140 feet above sea level, descends gradually until it crosses into Hillside at an elevation of 70 feet. The land east of the Elizabeth River is a gently rolling plain. To the west of the river, a spur of the Orange Mountains reaches 220 feet above sea level at Franklin Terrace.

The first inhabitants of the Elizabeth River valley were the Awkinges-awky or Hackensacks, a sub-tribe of the Lenni Lenape. No Native American village is known to have existed in Irvington, but the region's plentiful game and well-stocked streams suggests that the Hackensack made their camps here.

In 1666 several small vessels from Connecticut sailed up the Passaic River in search of a safe landing. Within a decade Newark's first settlers laid out highways, erected a meeting house, and established themselves on the banks of the river. The next generation looked to the west for additional land. There can be no doubt that Irvington was explored soon after Newark was formed: the Indian trail that later became Clinton Avenue led straight to the Elizabeth River and the open meadows of the valley. History has not preserved the name of Irvington's first European settler nor the date when he and his family cleared the woods to build the first rough cabin here. Tradition has it that Irvington was founded in 1692.

During the early years of the eighteenth century, a handful of families inhabited the valley, most of them clustered along the river. West Farms, as the place was originally called, gained its first citizen of note when Samuel Camp sold his property in Newark and moved his family here about 1725. His son, Joseph, opened a general store on what is now Clinton Avenue about 1740, farmed the family's lands, owned a sawmill on the river, and operated a cider mill and distillery on Vinegar Hill. At mid-century, Joseph Camp and his numerous relatives and descendants owned nearly one-third of the arable land in what is now Irvington, reason enough for West Farms to become known as Camp's Town.

The story of the American Revolution was played out in miniature in what was to become Irvington. Joseph Camp's son, Caleb, was a stalwart patriot. A member of the Provincial Congress, he served as a member of the General Assembly after independence was declared, as a member of the Council of Safety for eleven years, and as Speaker of the Assembly. His neighbor and sometime business partner, Samuel Hayes, earned his laurels during eight years as a major in the Essex County Militia. More than forty men from West Farms and vicinity served the American cause in the fight for independence.

Village life began to return to normal soon after the British were driven from New Jersey. Camptown built a new schoolhouse in 1809, saw it burn to the ground in 1826, and replaced it with a three-story brick building that was to stand as a landmark at the Center until 1913. The Camptown Academy was Irvington's only school until Central School on Clinton Avenue opened in 1870. A stagecoach line between Morristown and Jersey City began operating with a stop in Camptown in 1798. The new fast mail line from Philadelphia to New York City chose the village as a relay station in 1800.

By the mid-1800s Camptown had grown to a village of about nine hundred; most of its citizens were farmers, but a growing number of professional and business people from Newark, Jersey City, and New York City sought the place out for its quiet country lifestyle. When Stephen Foster published his new ballad, "De Camptown Races," in 1850, the "better folk" of the village were mortified that people would equate their hometown with the bawdy places and events celebrated in Foster's song. To Lydia Crawford, the wife of the local postmaster, belongs the laurels for choosing Camptown's new name: her 1852 suggestion, "Irvingtown," honored Washington Irving, America's greatest living man of letters.

Irvington sent nearly seventy of her sons to fight for the Union in the Civil War. Amos J. Cummings, sergeant major of the 26th New Jersey Volunteers, was the most decorated, winning the Congressional Medal of Honor for "distinguished gallantry."

On March 27, 1874, the State approved legislation that created "a body politic" known as the Village of Irvington. Until then only a section of Clinton Township, Irvington was now an independent municipality with its own mayor, village trustees, police department (1893), and fire department (1894). Laws approved in Trenton in 1903 and again in 1908 that would have joined Irvington to Newark were turned aside as local voters soundly rejected the idea of annexation.

By the turn of the century, Irvington had been transformed from a country village to a thriving middle-class suburb of Newark. The town's first electric trolley in 1890 was largely responsible. Throughout the period 1860 to 1890, when horse-drawn trolleys on Clinton and Springfield Avenues were the swiftest means of travel between Irvington and Newark, Irvington's population hovered between 1,500 and 2,000. By 1905, just fifteen years after the first electric trolleys plied Springfield Avenue, there were 7,180 people here, an increase of 239%. Irvington's development began gradually in the late 1880s, gained momentum at the turn of the century, and then skyrocketed during the twenty-five years between 1905 and 1930. Irvington's population was 11,877 in 1910. Ten years later, 25,480 people called the town their home, a 115% gain. By 1930 the number stood at 56,733, an amazing 125% increase. Since the building boom finally ended in 1930 after having consumed every farm and field in town, Irvington's population has remained relatively stable; although at a little over 3 square miles, Irvington is one of the most densely populated places in the state.

Census takers in 1905 found that one-fifth of Irvington's people were foreign-born, most of them natives of Germany, England, and Ireland. During the first three-quarters of the twentieth century, a wave of immigrants swept over Irvington. German-Americans bought or rented so heavily in the East Ward that from the 1880s to the 1950s they were the town's most dominant ethnic group. The town's Jewish community, numbering over nine thousand in the 1970s, was virtually non-existent until 1900. The largest ethnic group by the 1970s, Polish-Americans moved here in large numbers after World War I. Italian-Americans began arriving in the West Ward in the early 1940s, followed in the 1960s by Ukrainian-Americans who were four thousand strong when the 1970 census was taken.

Although the Irvington depicted in the photos which follow has changed significantly, its memory remains fresh in the minds of the untold thousands who have called the town "home."

One
Camptown Days

The Grist Mill on Union Avenue, *c.* 1904. Although tradition has it that Irvington was founded in 1692, settlement probably began in the mid-1680s. The gristmill near the sand pits (where today's Union Avenue becomes Mill Road) was the earliest of several mills powered by the limpid waters of the Elizabeth River.

Caleb Camp (1790–1872). He lived in the family homestead on Springfield Avenue near Lake Street, keeping a grocery store there as late as the Civil War. His ancestors moved to what was then known as West Farms, *c.* 1725.

Drake's Mill on the Elizabeth River, near Mill Road, *c.* 1890. It was the power of the river's currents, harnessed by saw, grain, and cider mills, and the fertile soil of the river valley that drew settlers here, including Joseph Camp. By the late 1700s, the tiny village was known as Camp's Town.

The Brick Academy on Clinton Avenue, 1858. During the Revolution, nearly forty men from Camptown, almost the entire adult male population, served the patriot cause. By 1809 Camptown had its first schoolhouse, replaced after a fire in 1826 by this handsome three-story structure.

David McMaster's home on the Plank Road, 1858. The pace of life quickened in the 1830s and 1840s when Camptown gained a new class of citizenry, wealthy businessmen who built their "country" homes along the Newark and Springfield Turnpike (today's Springfield Avenue) and the Plank Road (Clinton Avenue).

Cyrus Durand (1787–1868). Among the newcomers to Camptown, Durand was an inventor, silversmith, and engraver of national repute.

A Sample of Durand's Work, 1840. Called "one of America's most remarkable geniuses," Durand pioneered many anti-counterfeiting measures still used in security printing today.

Orchard Hill, 1858. Nathan J. Bailey's impressive mansion on Nye Avenue, corner of Nesbit Terrace, was built in 1840. Samuel Hewlett, the temperance lecturer, lived here in the 1870s with his daughter, Pochahantas, an opera singer. In 1901 the mansion became part of the Bethany Home for the Aged.

Rev. Isaac C. Goff (1808–1886). Camptown was without a house of worship until 1830, when Goff, then a twenty-two-year-old seminary graduate, became pastor of First Christian Church.

John N. Crawford. One of Camptown's foremost citizens in the years leading up to the Civil War, Crawford was postmaster, township clerk, founder of a literary journal, and merchant.

Crawford's Store and Residence, 1858. A bewildering variety of goods greeted customers at Crawford's general store on Union Avenue just south of today's Nye Avenue. Crawford carried just about everything imaginable, including carpets, window curtains, "segars," wall paper, and medicinal wines.

Residence of Rev. Moses Cummings, 1858. A lay preacher, dentist, and jeweler, Cummings (1816–1867) moved to Camptown in 1852. In 1855 he became editor of the *Christian Palladium*, a semi-monthly newspaper dedicated to the downfall of atheism, evolution, ignorance, and human slavery.

Congressman Amos J. Cummings, 1880. Rev. Cummings' son was a local boy made good. A Civil War hero and winner of the Medal of Honor, he was a long-time editor of the *New York Sun*, newspaper columnist, and eight-term congressman.

Page 23

CLINTON TAX.

Present this Bill.

Mr. George H Osborn

YOUR STATE, COUNTY, AND TOWNSHIP TAX FOR 1858, IS . . . . . . $ 5.90

YOUR DOG TAX IS . . . . . .

YOUR ROAD TAX IS 96

Received Payment, 6.86

R W Osborn COLLECTOR.

Now due, and payable to me before the 20th day of December next, or they will be returned according to law. The Court of Appeals in cases of Taxation will be held at the Irvington House, in Irvington, on the Fourth Tuesday in November next, at Two o'clock, P. M.

REUBEN W. OSBORN,

CLINTON, October 1, 1858.

☞ I may be found, December 13th, at Headley's Store, Middleville, from 2 till 5 o'clock, P. M.; December 14th, at Tate's Store, Lyon's Farms, from 1 till 5 o'clock, P. M.; December 15th, at Lyde's Store, Newark, from 8 A. M. till 4 o'clock, P. M.; December 16th, at Taylor's Store, South Orange, from 8 A. M. till 4 o'clock, P. M.; and from the 17th till the 20th, at my Office, in Irvington, where I will receive money for Taxes.

REUBEN W. OSBORN, *Collector.*

An 1858 Tax Bill. Camptown was merely an unincorporated village in Clinton Township, a sprawling chunk of geography that included present-day South Orange, Maplewood, Irvington, and almost all of Newark's South and Central Wards.

Washington Irving. Camptown became "Irvingtown" in 1852, honoring America's greatest living man of letters who was the creator of Rip Van Winkle and Ichabod Crane. To Lydia Crawford belongs the honor of suggesting the name in a contest sponsored by the Camptown Debating Society. "Clintonia" was one of the runner-ups.

Two

A Quiet Country Village

Irvington Center, looking east, *c.* 1880. Seventy men from Irvington fought for the Union in the Civil War. When they returned home, they found "a state gone wild over wealth and prosperity." The winds of change reached Irvington in 1868 when the horse-drawn trolley (seen here at the far right) linked Newark and Irvington. Wooden sidewalks were laid in 1874, followed a year later by gas lights. By 1880 population had reached an estimated two thousand, double what it was twenty years earlier.

The Elizabeth River near Drake's Lower Pond, 1898. The pace of change was gradual, however. Away from the center of town, where the Plank Road (Clinton Avenue) and the Turnpike (Springfield Avenue) intersected, with its hotel and handful of commercial buildings, life was still decidedly rural. The Elizabeth River followed its bucolic path to Staten Island Sound with little interruption.

The Dam at the Foot of Drake's Lower Pond. In this photo, taken about 1900, what would later be Union Place, Stewart, Lindsley and Harper Avenues is still covered with a thick stand of evergreens and oak trees. Village life was unhurried: In 1878 the governing body instructed the clerk to confiscate cows pastured on the roadways.

Drake's Upper Pond, *c.* 1885. Mahlon Drake's double-walled ice house, later the site of Irvington High School's athletic fields, provided employment to a score of ice cutters who labored for five weeks each winter, slicing the ice, floating it to the ice house, and packing it in sawdust for sale the next summer.

Drake's Lower Pond, *c.* 1895. Drake harvested ice in Irvington until 1904 when pollution signalled the end of his business. The upper and lower ponds, filled with soil from hundreds of newly excavated basements, became the Orange Avenue and Chancellor Avenue playgrounds, respectively.

The Methodist Church at Union and Nye Avenues, 1901. As the village's population grew to an estimated three thousand in 1890, the number of churches multiplied as well. The Methodist's building, erected by the Episcopalians in 1841, served the congregation from 1847 to 1968. Rev. John H. Vincent, who preached here during the Civil War, was founder of the Chautauqua movement.

The First Reformed Church, *c*. 1885. This handsome Greek Revival structure stood atop the Springfield Avenue hill at New Street (where Woolworth's is now) for eighty years. Rev. Henry Vehslage, who served as pastor from 1861 to 1894, was remembered at his death as "the pivotal center around which this community, socially and religiously, has revolved." He was Grand Master of the State Masons in 1883 and 1884.

St. Leo's Church in 1897. Irvington's Catholics were without parish or pastor until 1878, when St. Leo's was dedicated. Rev. Walter Fleming, the first pastor, bought a lot at the corner of Myrtle Avenue and Irvington Place and erected this small wooden chapel that served the congregation until 1926.

The Brick Academy, *c.* 1910. From 1826 to 1870 Irvington's school children crowded into the old Academy on Clinton Avenue (where Fidelity Union Bank later stood). So inadequate did it become that in 1870 villagers raised $22,000 and erected Central School, a massive brick-turreted structure that served until 1941.

Central School, 1898. Later known as Clinton Avenue School, the structure housed six hundred students and ten teachers when this view was taken. Conditions were so deplorable that the school board said the building needed to be "cleaned and thoroughly disinfected. But we have no money."

Rev. John L. Chapman (1812–1891). Pastor of the Reformed Church, crusader against slavery, leader of the education reform movement, author, and historian, "Old Dominie," as Rev. Chapman was fondly known, was a figure of commanding presence.

Elmwood, *c.* 1890. Cyrus Durand sold Elmwood to his son-in-law, Rev. Chaoman, in 1856 for $6,000, a goodly sum in those days. Rev. Chapman's mansion, which stood on what is now Chapman Place between Springfield and Elmwood Avenues, was the center of Irvington's cultural life for nearly sixty years.

Jane Wade Durand Chapman. Cyrus Durand's daughter outlived her husband, Rev. Chapman, by fourteen years, remaining at Elmwood until 1905 when she moved to Washington, D.C., to be near her son.

Elias Wade Durand (1824–1908). Son of Cyrus Durand, he was an inventor, landscape painter, gentleman farmer, and expert horticulturalist. His seedling strawberry, the "Great American," won a bronze medal at the 1876 Centennial Exposition.

C. Durand Chapman, 1889. Born in Irvington in 1856, this son of Rev. John Chapman is still remembered by art historians as one of New Jersey's finest late-nineteenth-century artists and illustrators.

The Irvington Art and Camera Club Outing, 1900. Founded in 1892, the club was Irvington's first association of artists. Among its members were painters Elias W. Durand, C. Durand Chapman, and Edward N. Griffith, photographer Julius Bartosch, and Will Crawford, one of the finest cartoonists of his era.

Reunion of the Irvington Base Ball Club, 1897. The Civil War was barely over when employees of Irvington's Belcher Rule Co. organized a baseball club. The "celebrated Irvington nine" played all the Newark clubs as well as the Elizabeth Resolutes, the Paterson Mystics, and the Bloomfield Oneidas. In 1866 nearly six thousand fans watched a match in Irvington between the home team and the New York Mutuals.

Phebe Chandler (1823–1907). Most Irvingtonians had little time for camera clubs and baseball matches. Mrs. Walter Chandler, seen here *c.* 1890, lived her entire life in Irvington, raising a family of ten.

Walter Burton Chandler (1826–1909). Shown here *c.* 1905 with one of his many grandchildren, Mr. Chandler sold milk door-to-door for over forty years, his career interrupted only by the nine months he served in the Union Army.

The Chandler Home, 1900. Photographed during the famous Irvington-Maplewood-Millburn Bicycle Race, the Chandler home at the corner of Clinton and Bruen Avenues was a plain Federal-style structure built *c.* 1828. A large pegged barn in the backyard housed the family's chickens and cows.

David S. Terrill. Irvington's first undertaker, Terrill went into business in 1867 during a time when funerals were still held in private homes. A veteran of the Civil War, Terrill poses here in a uniform a size or two larger than the one he wore in his soldiering days.

Irvington Center, 1896. This view looks east, with Springfield Avenue to the left and Clinton Avenue to the right. Note the trolley tracks on Springfield Avenue with the irons poles between the tracks from which the cables were hung. The high poles near the sidewalk were for Western Union while the small white poles held telephone and electric wires. The broom on top of the pole signifies a clean sweep for President McKinley in the November election.

Irvington Center, 1905. This is the same view ten years later, with new buildings, more utility poles, trolley tracks, and a street light where the McKinley broom pole once held sway.

Irvington Hotel, c. 1890. The hotel stood on the northwest corner of Springfield and Clinton Avenues for more than fifty years, until 1924 when it was demolished to make way for the Drake Building. It replaced an earlier hotel that had stood there before the Revolution. "Mug" Fagin is sweeping the sidewalk. Clinton Avenue School is to the right center.

Van Zandt's Coal & Wood Depot, c. 1890. Located on the southwest corner of Union and Springfield Avenues, Van Zandt's sold coal and wood for heating, axle grease for wagons, and baled hay, straw, oats, and corn for horses.

A Bucolic Scene, *c.*1885. A hundred years ago Irvington was still very much a rural suburb of Newark, as this photo taken in the vicinity of what would become Chancellor Playground attests. The view is north, with the Elizabeth River out of sight at the far left.

The Old Swimming Hole, 1910. These boys are swimming in the Elizabeth River, behind the future site of Union Avenue School. The level area behind them would become Chancellor Playground. The river, then cool and inviting, is now trapped in a concrete tunnel beneath the Garden State Parkway.

Three

A Population of Good Citizens

Village Trustees, 1894. Not until March 1874 was Irvington set off from Clinton Township as a separate and independent municipality. On April 18, 1874, William Hayes Murphy, a Newark industrialist who lived in a 13-room mansion on Myrtle Avenue, was elected village president. Three of the village's five trustees—William A. Reeve (left), Henry L. Leibe (center), and Gottlob Kautzman (right)—sit for the photographer in this very serious 1894 view.

The Balloon Ascension, 1893. Irvington's development as a middle-class suburb of Newark began gradually in the 1880s, gained momentum at the turn of the century, and then skyrocketed during the next quarter century. Nicholas Weber and George Garwood opened a 300-lot tract on Myrtle Avenue in 1892, selling two-thirds of the lots within two years for $200 each. This hot-air balloon ascent in 1893 drew customers from far and wide.

A Row of Cottages, *c.* 1890s. These "neat cottages" on Cummings Street were typical of the houses beginning to displace Irvington's farmers. Manhattan Park, the first major development, covered some 20 acres of farmland to the west of Grove Street. Builders and developers, such as Aaron Rodwell, William Allen, Halsey Tichenor, Frederick and Franklin Eckelhofer, and Edgar Bross, are remembered today by the streets that bear their names.

Laying Trolley Tracks on Springfield Avenue, *c.* 1890. Irvington's transformation from rural village to city suburb was due chiefly to improved transportation links with downtown Newark. Horse-drawn trolleys made their appearance on Clinton Avenue in 1863. In 1890, when the electric trolley supplanted horses on the Springfield Avenue line, a squad of police had to be called out to keep curious crowds away from the tracks.

A Springfield Avenue Trolley, 1905. Consolidated Traction Co. ran the Springfield Avenue line until bought out by Public Service Corporation. Passengers, as well as the U.S. Mail, could make the trip from Irvington to Newark in less than thirty minutes.

The Last of the Cattle, *c.* 1905. Dairy cattle belonging to Will Harrison pose for the photographer at the corner of Springfield Avenue and Grove Street. New homes and barns cover the fields to the northeast.

Home Sweet Home, *c.* 1895. The Brandenburg family stand proudly in front of their new three-story Queen Anne-style home at the corner of Orange Avenue and Rich Street. Sidewalks and curbs, a rarity in Irvington, marked this as an affluent neighborhood.

Scuffletown, 1905. This modest house at 110 Berkshire Place was built to plans drawn by Peter Anton Ehrhardt, a carpenter and farmer. He and his wife, Margaret, and their two children, Willie and Alma, pose out front. Their capacious barn, grape arbor, fruit trees, and a tiny outhouse dimly visible at far left complete the picture.

The Weber Mansion, 1906. This 16-room house at 660 Stuyvesant Avenue was built in 1906 by Nicholas Weber of Weber Baking Co. fame. At one time Irvington's largest taxpayer, Weber, his wife, Louisa, and their sixteen children lived here until 1925. After 1926 the building served as the Terrill Funeral Home.

The Glorieux Mansion, *c.* 1900. A magnificent example of Gothic Revival style, William L. Glorieux's home at 944 Clinton Avenue (now the site of the Public Service building) was built in the 1850s. This 22-room house featured Walnut woodwork, imported carved marble fireplaces, and acres of formal gardens. Glorieux, his wife Eleanor, their children Philip and Jean, and their coachman, Napoleon Depue, look contentedly into the camera.

William L. Glorieux (1854–1924). Mayor of Irvington for fifteen years between 1898 and 1917, Glorieux was one of Irvington's wealthiest citizens; he was co-owner of the Irvington Smelting & Refining Works on Nye Avenue.

Julius Bartosch (1847–1933). At one time or another, almost everyone had a portrait taken by photographer Bartosch, many of whose photographs illustrate this book.

Bartosch's Studio, *c.* 1895. On Springfield Avenue next to the Drake Apartments, Bartosch's studio and home stood just west of the Irvington Hotel. The hotel's sheds, visible at the rear, echoed to the sounds of cow auctions every other Monday afternoon until the eve of World War I.

The Drake Apartments, *c.* 1915. Still standing, these apartments built by Mahlon S. Drake in the 1890s were only the first of several commercial structures built by members of the Drake family in Irvington Center. It was Drake who replaced the old Irvington Hotel with a $100,000 office and retail building in 1925.

The Loehnberg Mansion, 1898. Yet another of Irvington's grand homes was this mansion built by Louis Loehnberg, a retired Newark manufacturer. On Clinton Avenue not far from Mayor Glorieux's home, the Loehnberg place sported a gazebo, water fountain, flower beds, and wrought-iron fence.

This Brew's For You, *c.* 1900. For the men of Irvington village, the many neighborhood saloons, which were outfitted with free lunches and good companionship, were favorite places to relax. George Bonnet and Philip Popper, posing here, owned the Stuyvesant House at the northeast corner of Springfield and Stuyvesant Avenues.

All Aboard, 1907. An all-Irvington trip up the Hudson River to College Point aboard the *Commander* was a summer highlight for many. Women and children are conspicuous by their absence.

A Church Picnic, 1906. Members of the First Christian Church are photographed as they get ready to leave for a Sunday picnic, possibly as far from Irvington as Millburn's Hemlock Falls or the Eagle Rock in West Orange.

Walker at the Wheel, *c.* 1910. Joseph Walker's factory on the corner of Springfield Avenue and Lake Street was the only one in town when it opened in 1883. One of the first in Irvington to own an automobile, Walker is shown here taking some friends on a Sunday excursion.

Irvington Field Club Base Ball Team, 1889. Baseball and football were the town's most popular sports, played wherever there was an open field. The Field Club's confident-looking club included, from left to right: (standing) Stoutenburgh, McKee, Philip Becker, Mills, and Frank Weber; (sitting in center rear) Charlie Sweezey; and (sitting in front) Wally Bennett, Adam Joeck, and unknown. Unknown, too, is the young ball boy's name.

Role Reversal, 1915 Style. Olympic Park was Irvington's favorite amusement spot from the day it opened in May 1904. Here the New Jersey Association of Police Chiefs gathers for dinner at the park on May 6, 1915, dressed as convicts. Herman H. A. Schmidt, the park's owner, is the man standing at the rear dressed as the warden.

The Start, 1896. For nearly twenty years the annual Memorial Day bicycle race on Springfield and Clinton Avenues through Irvington, Maplewood, and Millburn was one of the leading cycle contests in the nation. At its height, thirty thousand people lined the 25-mile course. The scratch group waits for the signal to take off in this photo snapped at the eleventh annual race.

The Finish, 1896. According to the *New York Recorder*, nearly twenty thousand men, women, and children viewed the 1896 race along "the five-mile stretch of macadam running through the beautiful rolling countryside." Winner of the race was Robert Alexander of Connecticut. Monte Scott of Rhode Island won the time prize with 1 hour, 8 minutes and 29 seconds.

Cookin' Good Music, 1914. The Irvington Methodist Church's Kitchen Band entertained the flock with musical instruments pieced together from funnels, sifters, pots and pans, a broom, and other assorted kitchen utensils.

Edwin Kulp, Editor, 1894. Irvington's first successful weekly newspaper was *The Record*, published in 1894 and 1895.

Anthony Oliver, *c.* 1900. Only a handful of blacks lived in Irvington at the turn of the century. Oliver was a deliveryman for N. Drake & Co.

Samuel Lemmerman (1864–1952). A native of Russia, he was one of the first Jews to live in Irvington, opening a small dairy on Mill Road in 1898.

An Unhappy Crew, 1906. The photographer must have forgotten to say "cheese" when he posed this group of children in their pony wagon. From left to right are Elmer, Alice, Anna, and Walter Andruss.

Walter Hardgrove (1889–1918). Growing up in Irvington was not easy when your parents made you dress like this, even if you were only five.

Mabel G. Chandler (1901–1987). Born in a house across the street from the Irvington Smelting & Refining Co. where her father worked, she graduated from the eighth grade at Augusta Street School in June 1915.

Florence Avenue School. Irvington's population growth placed enormous pressures on the school system, with students outstripping facilities no matter what the Board of Education did. Florence Avenue School, seen here in a 1927 photo, eased the pressure somewhat when it was completed in 1899.

Coit Street School. After it opened in 1901, the Board of Education was finally able to abandon a two-story frame building at Grove Street and 14th Avenue that it had rented to meet school demands in the Manhattan Park section of town. Coit Street School was to be closed as an economy measure in 1935 and torn down in 1939.

Mount Vernon Avenue School. A few rooms in a rented chapel at the corner of Lyons and Chester Avenues were all the school board could muster for Scuffletown students until 1908, when it built this school in the Spanish-style then so popular.

First Grade, Florence Avenue School, 1908. Frederick A. Frost, standing in the second row from the top with the cap pulled down over his eyes, remembered that Principal Sarah Jane Betts (rear, center) was nicknamed "Betsy the Terror"—behind her back, of course.

Class of 1917. Augusta Street School opened in 1913 with Mae Connor (standing, at far right) at the helm. Only about 20% of the eighth-grade Class of 1917 shown here went on to Irvington High School, then sharing Madison Avenue School. The rest began their working careers.

Town Hall, 1895. For twenty years Irvington's village trustees met in the Odd Fellow's Hall above J.T. Castle's Ice Cream Store. On September 2, 1895, the new town hall was dedicated "with the grandest public celebration ever given." The fire department occupied the first floor, while the police and municipal government were located on the second and third.

Emanuel United Church of Christ, 1898. This frame building on the corner of Nye Avenue and Lincoln Place has housed Irvington's first German-language church since 1898. Not until World War I was English used in services.

Clinton Avenue from the Center, looking east, 1902. To the left is the Glorieux Building, now the site of the Public Service building and bus terminal. In the photograph's center is the steeple of the First Christian Church, torn down in the mid-1950s to make way for the Garden State Parkway.

Springfield Avenue, *c.* 1905. This is a view of the northerly side of Springfield Avenue west of Clinton Avenue with the old Irvington Hotel, its cow barns, and the Drake apartments where druggist Harry McDavit sold everything from perfumes and stationery to Cascaret for a sour stomach, Cal-Cura Solvent for gall stones, and Indian Vegetable Pills for the nervous.

Union Avenue, c. 1900. Union Avenue south of Nye Avenue was almost all residential, with sidewalks, curbs, and a Telfordized roadway (crushed trap rock rolled smooth) that turned into a muddy miasma during rainy periods. In 1898, when Irvington became a town, there was not a single paved thoroughfare.

Orange Avenue, c. 1900. In 1894 the local newspaper reported, "loud complaints over the condition of the village streets, which daily grow worse. . . . Nearly all the main driving thoroughfares are now in a state that is nearly impassable. . . . The mountain stone which has been placed on the roads lays loose on the surface and no amount of rolling will make a solid roadbed."

Clinton Avenue, near Coit Street. Clinton Avenue gained distinction in 1905 as the first paved roadway when it was cobblestoned from the Center to the Newark line. Clinton Avenue near Coit Street was lined with spacious homes in this photo taken *c.* 1910.

Springfield Avenue at 43rd Street, *c.* 1910. By the first decade of the twentieth century, many of the buildings that even today line Springfield Avenue had been erected. Hosp's Hotel, the turreted building seen here to the left, catered to Olympic Park visitors. Springfield Avenue was still not paved from the Newark to Maplewood line.

Four

The Spirit of Enterprise

Harvesting Strawberries, *c.* 1905. Throughout the eighteenth and nineteenth centuries, agriculture was the town's chief business; not until the post-World War I building boom were the last of the farmers driven into retirement. Here Charles Momm supervises a curiously well-dressed crew harvesting strawberries on his farm west of Stuyvesant Avenue.

Stuyvesant Avenue near Lyons Avenue, *c.* 1900. The Dorer family owned a large tract of land south of Lyons Avenue and east of Stuyvesant, all of which they farmed intensively. Here milk wagons line up to load the day's deliveries. Dairy farms dotted the landscape: in 1914 there were eighteen dairies still operating within town limits.

The Village Smithy, *c.* 1890. Early industry catered to the farmers and dairymen who owned most of Irvington's arable land. George Meeker's blacksmith shop on Clinton Avenue just east of the Academy was a busy place in this Gay Nineties view.

Joseph T. Castles (1862–1938). His confectionary and cigar store at the Center was a landmark for many years. In the mid-1890s Castles went into the ice cream business using a recipe for frozen cream that Elias W. Durand had concocted.

J.T. Castles' Ice Cream Store, 1901. Later the site of the Castle Theatre, Castles' store is draped in black bunting for the death of President William McKinley in this view. The Odd Fellows' Hall upstairs did double duty as the town hall for both Irvington and Clinton Township.

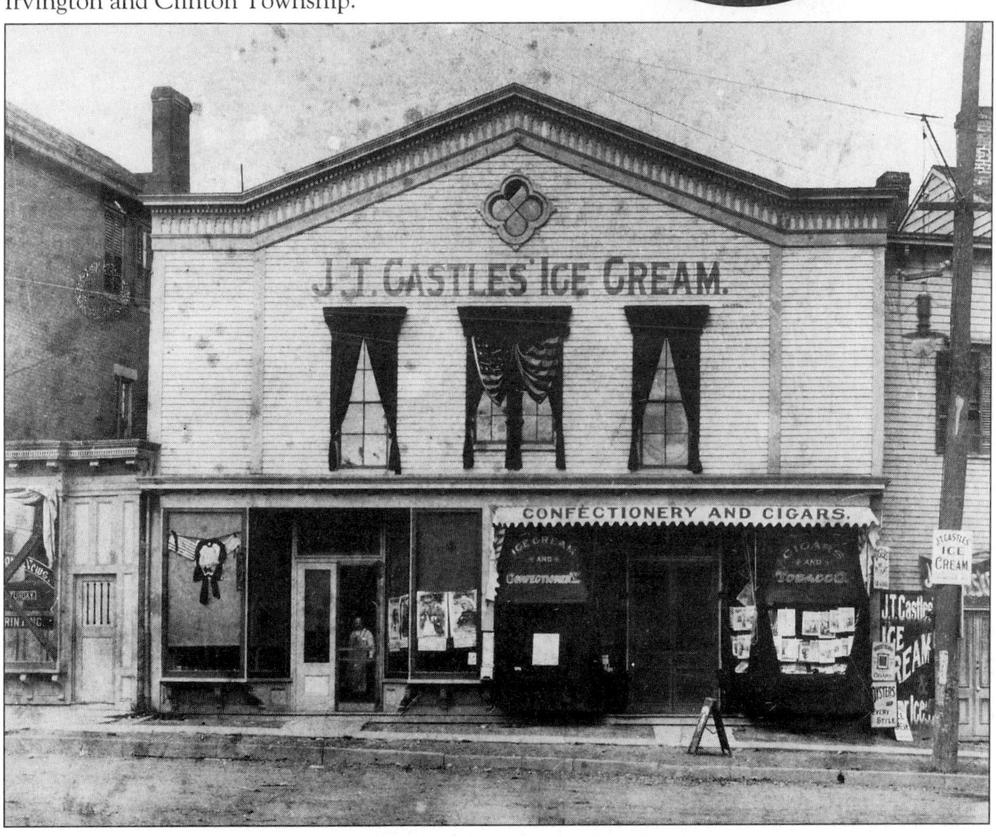

May We Serve You? George Lacey, at left, and M.C. Crane, at right, await the day's customers in this *c.* 1920 view of Castles' Ice Cream Store. Cigars, film, and confectionery beckoned customers much as they do today.

Nicholas H. Weber in 1906. He moved from Newark to Irvington in 1884 to start the first bakery in town.

The Weber Baking Co. Located in a three-story building at 1021 Springfield Avenue, Weber's bakery prospered almost from the start. Horse-drawn delivery wagons, shown here lined up in front of the bakery, sold his products door-to-door throughout Essex County.

A Necessary Business. David S. Terrill, Irvington's first undertaker and embalmer, awaits his customers at 1019 Springfield Avenue, next door to the bakery. "All orders promptly attended to, night and day," promised Terrill's newspaper ads.

Attending to Orders, 1892. Charles Hoyt Terrill, seated at left, succeeded his father in the business. His son, W. Clifton Terrill, seated at right, followed his father's footsteps. C.H. Terrill, appointed in 1901, did double duty as Irvington postmaster for many years. His son was president of Clinton Cemetery from 1924 to 1964.

L.A. Apgar's Meat Market, 1904. Fresh poultry and fresh and cured meats await the day's customers. Sawdust on the floor absorbed the drippings. Rib roast was 12¢ a pound, chickens were 14¢ a pound, and then as now sirloin was the most expensive cut at 18¢.

Bruck & Mury, 1906. Indoor plumbing and heating created a demand for plumbers, a trade unheard of only a few years before. From left to right are: (seated) unknown, Red Oxley, Fred Underwood, Mr. Sidner, George Schaeffer, and Jimmie; (rear) Gus Bischof, Al Rademacher, E. Boyer Mury, Joe Bruck, and Fred Schneider. Harry Nungesser holds the bicycle.

J.E. Mergott, *c*. 1895. "In the eastern part of town, on a hill which overlooks the greater part of the town, stands a group of factories . . . destined to form the centre of a big manufacturing district," wrote *The Record* in 1894. Mergott's on Coit Street specialized in brass novelties.

Weiner Manufacturing Co., 1912. Saddlery hardware was the specialty of this machine shop, typical of the small factories that dotted Enterprise Hill. Each machine was connected by overhead belts to a central power station, making for a noisy and dangerous environment.

Irvington Smelting & Refining Co., 1898. Sixty men labored around the clock at the highest wages then paid in the precious metals refining industry. In 1894 Glorieux and Woolsey installed huge dynamos that illuminated the factory and powered the refiners. The dynamos had been exhibited at the World's Columbian Exposition in 1893.

Irvington National Bank. Irvington's first bank opened its doors at the intersection of Clinton and Springfield Avenues in 1906. William L. Glorieux was the bank's first and only president until his death in 1924. Nathaniel Drake, Theodore Gerth, Charles Baker, Joseph T. Castles, Nicholas Weber, Harry Durand, Adrian Riker, Ernest Boerger, Edmund Sargeant, and J.B. Woolsey were the incorporators of the bank, which was merged into the Fidelity Union Trust Co. in 1949.

Irvington's First Wrecker, 1918. Dr. Albion C. Christian, who lived and practiced at the corner of Ball Street and Clinton Avenue, bought Irvington's first automobile, a shiny black Winton, in 1900. Alexander Brunner opened the town's first automobile repair shop in 1905.

Picnic Bound, 1925. The Lionel Corporation moved to a plant on 21st Street in 1917. During its heyday, the electric toy train was America's most popular toy and Lionel was the most popular brand. Employees celebrated with a picnic in the country two years before the company moved to a new factory on Sager Place.

Irvington Varnish & Insulator Co., *c.* 1935. Located between Grove Street and Eastern Parkway, Irvington Varnish was Irvington's biggest manufacturing business. From 1906 to 1960, when it closed its doors, the company made varnished paper, cambrics and silks, plastic tubing, and brake linings. The 3M company acquired the plant in 1953 for $7 million.

Five

To Serve the People

The Pickle Barrel, 1894. Hastily-summoned bucket brigades became a thing of the past in the spring of 1894 when village trustees approved the purchase of the town's first fire apparatus for $225 and authorized a volunteer fire department of twenty men. Village trustee William R. Adams, who spearheaded the drive, is pictured here with the chemical apparatus, nicknamed the "Pickle Barrel." The dog, which answered to the name "Damn You," belonged to Nat Squire, a village character.

The New Hose Cart. In August 1894, village trustees doubled the size of the department and agreed to the purchase of this hose cart, a beautiful piece of apparatus decorated with silver bells, from the Hoboken department for $250. Edward D. Tuttle, who had worked with Adams, was named department foreman.

Horse-Drawn Hook and Ladder, Memorial Day Parade, 1909. Irvington's volunteers acquired their first horses in 1905, but since none were stabled in the fire stations, it now took longer to respond to alarms. There were five fire stations by 1906.

Chief Jonah Hardgrove. Head of the fire department from 1897 to 1904, Hardgrove poses here with a silver trumpet, the nineteenth century's version of the bullhorn.

The Jenny Lind, 1908. A paid fire department became a reality in 1908 when town fathers disbanded the volunteers "with thanks for their honorable service" and authorized a paid chief, driver, and assistant driver and forty volunteer call men. A Knox combination motorized apparatus affectionately known as the "Jenny Lind" entered service.

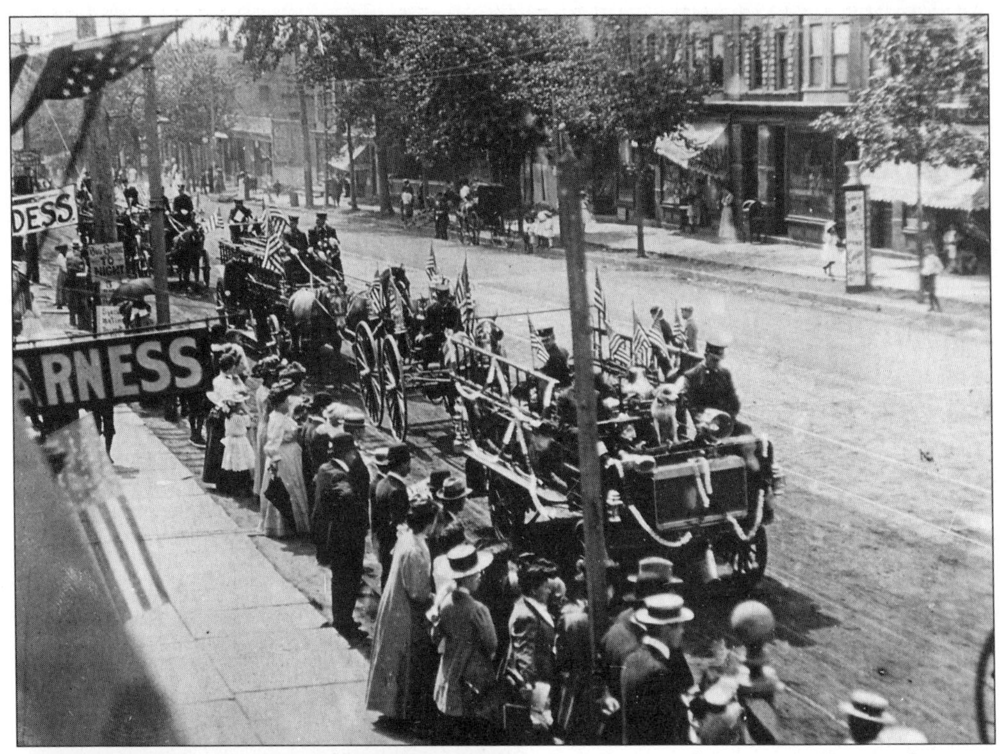

Parading on the Avenue. Exempt firemen parade down Springfield Avenue on Memorial Day 1914 with a combination of horse-drawn and motorized equipment. Irvington's best equipment was housed in Town Hall on Clinton Avenue until 1911 when the new central fire house on Washington Avenue was completed.

Thomas H. Kirkbride (1862–1939). A milkman and volunteer fireman, Kirkbride later transferred to the police department. He became chief in 1922.

Coit Street Fire House and Platoon, *c.* 1926. Under the leadership of Commissioner Leonard Setaro, Irvington's fire department became the first in the state to be entirely motorized. The American LaFrance aerial truck at left went into service in 1923.

Up to Their Knees in Water. Firemen are seen here battling an especially stubborn fire at the Lehigh Valley coal hoppers just off Clinton Avenue near the Newark line in this mid-1930s photo.

Stalwart Policemen Three, *c.* 1894. Irvington's first regular police officer was Constable Jeremiah Allen, appointed in 1888 for Sunday duty only. Six years later, when he was named superintendent of police, Allen headed a force of four men stationed on the first floor of the new Town Hall. Posing here are, from left to right, Walter Dixon, Jeremiah Allen, and Morton Smith.

James G. Mayfield. When the town of Irvington was incorporated in 1898, he was appointed the first chief of police.

A Paid Department, 1905. Three years after the town council established a paid police department, the force stood for this photo in front of the Town Hall. From left to right are: Sgt. Alexander Greene, William Vliet, Frank Elliott, Thomas H. Kirkbride, Leonard Shrock, William Romaine, Louis Allendorf, William Ruppee, Chief John Coleman, and Special Officer Edward Bataille.

Alexander Greene. He served as the town's chief of police from 1905 to 1922.

The New Headquarters, 1913. Completed at a cost of $20,000, the police department's new headquarters on Washington Avenue was dedicated in 1913. A central switchboard connected to twelve call boxes linked patrolmen on the beat to headquarters for the first time. Chief Greene, standing at left, led a force of sixteen men.

The Flapper Cop, 1926. Automobile traffic burgeoned in the post-World War I years, bringing 59 traffic accidents in 1921 alone. This traffic control booth stood at the intersection of Springfield and Clinton Avenues.

Irvington's Bulletproof Car, 1925. With the coming of Prohibition, a vast new field of criminal activity lay open for exploitation. Irvington police responded with an armor-plated car equipped with a double-barreled shot gun, gas bombs, and triple-thick glass. Police Commissioner Leonard Setaro proudly points to a bullet hole in the glass.

Circus Duty, 1935. When Irvington police weren't chasing bootleggers or bank robbers, they did crowd control duty at Ollemar Field while the circus came to town. Officer Gus Zelles stops for a moment on Springfield Avenue near the circus tents.

"Old Dead-Eye Coleman." In May 1940 Sgt. Andrew Coleman fired one shot, capturing four youthful bandits. A few years before this incident, Coleman had been police chief, only to be suspended and indicted in the infamous slot-machine scandal. A jury that deliberated only three hours found Coleman not guilty.

School Safety Patrol, 1926. Lacking enough manpower to patrol every hazardous intersection during school hours, Commissioner Setaro (saluting, at far left) organized a school safety patrol, one of the first in the nation.

Irvington General Hospital, *c.* 1926. Under the leadership of Walter S. Gray and Mayor Edward R. Folsom, the town's first modern hospital took form on 11 acres of farmland purchased from William L. Glorieux. Costing $350,000, the Tudor-style facility opened in March 1924.

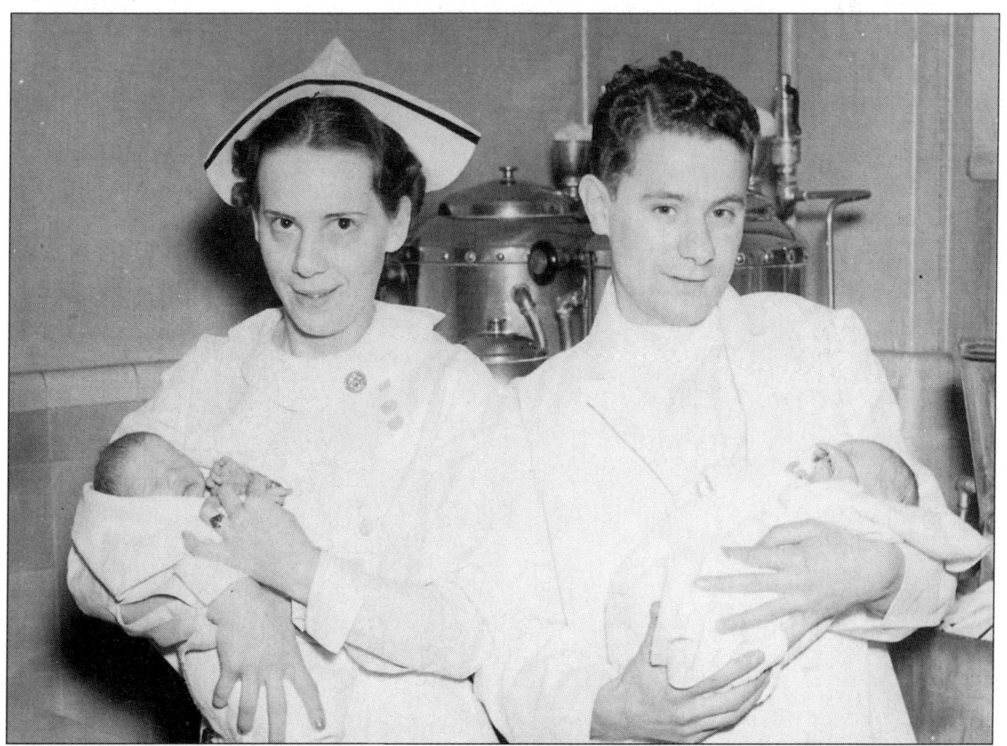

St. Patrick's Day Twins, 1937. One of only two municipally-owned hospitals in New Jersey, "IGH" was the birthplace of thousands of Irvingtonians. Here, Dr. Frank Glassner and Nurse Schumacher show off twins Robert and Joseph Damiano, born on March 17, 1937, to Joseph and Antoinette Damiano of Fern Avenue.

May E. Baillet, *c.* 1935. Fresh out of library school when she was appointed library director in 1915, Ms. Baillet served until June 1953.

Seven New Street, 1940. The library moved from Nye Avenue to New Street to a garage on Clinton Avenue before it found its new home on Civic Square in 1967. In this photo, Mary Kapala, the librarian, checks out books for Gertrude Koch and Carmen Baltz.

Six

Irvington Comes of Age

Polish Troops Camped in Irvington, 1916. Irvington's transformation from country village to city suburb, already well-underway when World War I broke out, was nearly complete by the time the war was over. Polish National Guard troops rest in their tents on the Speedway before departing for Europe in this 1916 photo.

Leaving for Camp Dix, 1917. While the war was confined to Europe, Irvington's Irish could jeer the British and her Germans could toast the Kaiser, all in perfect safety. When America entered the war in 1917, it was time to pull together: a total of 1,032 men served in the armed services during the war. Some are seen here leaving for Camp Dix from the Clinton Avenue railhead.

Who's Got the Liberty Button, 1917. By the end of the war, Irvingtonians had purchased $1.7 million worth of war bonds, or 130% of its quota. Town women not busy selling liberty bonds (pictured here) joined the local Red Cross and other service organizations.

Welcome Home, 1919. The town officially welcomed home its veterans on July 14, 1919, with a parade (seen here, at the Center) and banquet at Olympic Park. The twenty-six men from Irvington who made the ultimate sacrifice are memorialized in the names of streets opened after 1921.

Maypole Dance at Irvington Playground, 1920. Irvington's population virtually exploded during the second decade of the century, growing from 12,000 in 1910 to 25,500 in 1920. Developers of Laurel Avenue and Grant and Sherman Places advertised lots at $275, with $10 down and $5 per month.

Miniature Sailboat Race, Irvington Park, 1920. The war in Europe slowed the building boom only briefly. New construction, which averaged more than $1 million per year before the war, increased to $10 million per year after the war. The Wills place on Orange Avenue, one of the last farms left in town, was sold to developers in 1924.

Frank H. Morrell (1846–1924). Affectionately known to generations of students as "Daddy" Morrell, he guided Irvington's public school system as principal and superintendent of schools for forty-nine years.

Seventh Grade Class, Augusta Street School, *c.* 1925. The school system groaned under the pressure of new students, but leaders such as Morrell and Robert L. Saunders, superintendent from 1917 to 1934, held it together. Girls in this photo display their needles and thread while the boys get ready to enter the age of electricity.

Augusta Street School, Class of 1924. Helen Graham, teacher, at left, and Mae Connor, principal, at right, flank a class of eighth graders every bit as serious as the slogan they display.

Irvington High School Baseball, 1924. Even before Frank H. Morrell High School opened in 1926, Irvington produced many fine sports teams. The Class of 1924, the next to last high school class to attend Madison Avenue School, cheered a baseball team shown here coached by William B. Matthews, back row, fourth from left.

High School Debate Team, 1924. Pictured here, from left to right, are: (front row) Ruth Bach, Martha Tuckley, Emma Makinson, Emma Rausch, and Elsie Laroche; (back row) Frank Penl, Kenneth McClinchie, Clayton Haveron, and Henry Arnold.

Clinton Avenue School, *c.* 1922. Central School, better known as Clinton Avenue School, served the town until 1941. Converted into a community building, it was in use until 1972.

Hebrew School Outing, 1923. The Irish who settled here in the 1850s and 1860s were Irvington's first foreign-born. Soon they were followed by the Germans in the 1880s and the Jews a decade later. Max LeBow, first president of Temple B'nai Israel on Nye Avenue, stands at left, wearing a bow tie.

St. Leo's Roman Catholic Church, 1926. Built at a cost of a quarter of a million dollars, St. Leo's was dedicated in 1926. Rev. John O. Buchmann, who served the parish from 1928 to 1965, oversaw an ambitious building program that included a grammar school and high school named in honor of Newark's first archbishop.

First Baptist Church, 1920. The history of Irvington's First Baptist Church began in July 1917 when twenty-six men and women gathered for evening services. Three years later, they had erected this fine structure at the corner of Nye Avenue and Nesbit Terrace.

The Pilgrims Have Landed, 1926. On July 4, 1926, the town's school children marched down Springfield Avenue in a parade celebrating the 150th anniversary of the signing of the Declaration of Independence. Students from Augusta Street School shown here honored the Mayflower Pilgrims.

Edward R. Folsom, 1920. Mayor of Irvington from 1917 to 1923, he committed suicide rather than reveal a past that included a three-year prison term.

An Early Jitney, *c.* 1918. The first buses, called jitneys then, appeared on Irvington streets in 1915 when two enterprising young men painted that now-obsolete word on their automobile windshield and began cruising the streets offering 5¢ rides. Babe Germond, at left, and Bill Quinton pose with their jitney, one of the first made especially for public transportation.

When Hats Were in Style, 1923. The Alpha Class of the First Christian Church wore a bedazzling variety of wide-brimmed chapeaux in this November 1923 photo. Their teacher, Fannie Townsend, is fifth from left, front row.

Me and My Packard, 1924. Itinerant photographers toured the town's neighborhoods, offering to photograph children sitting in toy autos or on ponies. Seven-year-old Edward J. Oleksik of Ellis Avenue, shown here, later became chief and director of the Irvington Police Dept.

Carl J. Perina, 1929. Captain of the 1926 Frank H. Morrell High School football team, Perina went on to All-American honors at the University of Pennsylvania. He retired in 1980 as the town's director of parks and playgrounds.

A Teenage Flapper, 1921. Alma Ehrhardt (1903–1988) epitomizes the Flapper Era in this studio portrait taken when she was eighteen.

Preparing for the Memorial Day Parade, 1925. Organized in 1911, Irvington Lodge No. 1245, B.P.O.E., occupied this impressive clubhouse opposite Oraton Parkway until 1945. In later years this was known as The Ivanhoe (which Frank Dailey managed for nearly nine years) and The Coronet.

Memorial Day Parade, 1928. Little Miss Gloria Wallenberg stands on this float jointly sponsored by the Kiwanis Club and Irvington Garden Club. The house whose lawn the girl is watering is a model of the Servicemen's Club House on Springfield Avenue as it appeared when the town presented it to veterans' organizations in 1921.

First Cherry Tree, 1930. John Metzger, left, longtime president of the Garden Club, admires the first cherry tree planted at the Servicemen's Club House. Metzger was equally well known as Irvington's Mr. Santa Claus.

St. Paul's Lutheran Church, 1935. Services were held in this small frame building at the corner of 41st Street and Prospect Avenue from 1921 until May 1957, when Lutherans, then under the name Redeemer, dedicated their new building on 40th Street. M.A.L. Hirsch was the pastor when this photo was taken.

Girls' Athletic Club, 1937. Irvington's high school athletic teams were the envy of the state during the Twenties and Thirties. Advisors Mable Apple and Catherine MacGowan pose with club members Adeline Cimurro, Doris Steitz, Jean Kremer, and Grace McCloskey.

Mr. Baseball, 1934. John "Doc" Gantz, high school baseball mentor from 1929 to 1953, compiled a 436–97 record over his career. He surveys a practice with Captain Vito Miele.

Chancellor Arms, 1929. A scattering of multi-story brick apartment houses broke a skyline otherwise uniform with one-, two-, and three-family houses. This 38-family apartment, built in 1929, still stands at the corner of Chancellor Avenue and Lincoln Place. Irvington's building boom attracted neither the rich nor the poor, drawing instead the middle-class who considered a home in Irvington a step upward.

No. 15 Thirty-Eighth Street, 1927. The heady days of real estate development were over in Irvington when the Depression struck. This 40-family apartment was one of the last of its kind to be built in town. When it was finished in 1927, it catered to a "better class" that demanded larger apartments in the finest neighborhoods.

No. 159 Park Place, *c.* 1925. Typical of the best single-family houses built after World War I, this brick Colonial with tile roof, two-car garage, shutters, and shade trees, graced the corner of Park Place and Yale Avenue. Park Place, Lincoln Place, and Nesbit Terrace were initially developed by Nicholas Weber.

Everything Old is New Again, 1928. Standard Oil's gasolene station, at the corner of Lyons Avenue and Ball Street, sports a canopy over the pumps, a feature that stations are installing today.

Irvington Center, *c.* 1935. This row of stores on the north side of Springfield Avenue from New Street to Orange Avenue includes the Big Chief department store in the Rogosin Building. Maurice Rogosin opened a store at the Center in 1911, built the building that bears his name in 1925, and retired to California a wealthy man in 1935.

Irvington Center, 1939. The Irvington National Bank with its clock and flagpole anchors the corner of Springfield and Clinton Avenues behind the "Flapper Cop" in this photo looking east. The Public Service building on Clinton Avenue towers above the skyline in the distance.

Schraft's Pharmacy, *c.* 1929. A familiar landmark at the corner of Springfield and Stuyvesant Avenues until it moved a few blocks east in the 1950s, Schraft's stood opposite the Irvington Trust Co., the town's second bank.

Chancellor Avenue School, *c.* 1926. Built in 1914 and added to in 1926, Chancellor towers over the West Ward. Principals have included Sara Betts, Orville Staley, Willard Diffendafer, Dr. Ralph K. Turp, Dr. Harry Donovan, and Norman F. Gierman.

Used Car Heaven, *c.* 1940. The north side of Springfield Avenue from the Newark line to Oraton Parkway was lined with used car lots, one of the few places in town where such vaguely "disreputable businesses" were permitted. Most of the lots disappeared in the 1950s, although a few still linger there today.

No. 25 Springfield Avenue Trolley, near Schraft's Pharmacy, February 1934. Electric trolleys dominated mass transportation from 1890 to 1937, when both the Clinton and Springfield Avenue lines switched to all-service vehicles. Once the public lost its fear of electrocution, riders used trolleys not only to get to work in Newark and other cities, but for weekend and holiday pleasure outings as well.

No. 13 Broad Street Trolley at the Elmwood Loop, February 1934. Sunday outings became fashionable for a generation that fell in love with the trolley's breathtaking speed and natural air conditioning. Day trips to Trenton, Perth Amboy, Eagle Rock, and the Caldwell mountains were delights. Barely visible at right in this photo is the predecessor to Kless' Diner.

All-Service Vehicle, 1936. Irvington said a final farewell to its trolleys in September 1937 when the Clinton Avenue line switched to this all-service vehicle that ran on tracks, but could lower its pole and switch to a gasolene engine when necessary. Fully-motorized buses were only a few years away.

The Elk's Club, 1940. Across Springfield Avenue from the Elk's Club was Oraton Parkway (its entrance is visible here in the foreground), a band of greenery that stretched to Park Avenue in East Orange. In spring, motorists cruised the parkway, enjoying the Japanese cherry trees that lined the route. Oraton Parkway was destroyed when the Garden State Parkway cut through Irvington.

Walter S. Gray, *c.* 1930. Founder, publisher, and editor of the *Irvington Herald* from 1912 until his death in 1956, he also served as county freeholder and supervisor.

Milton Hammer, *c.* 1936. Sports columnist and cartoonist for the *Herald*, he was also a well-known radio commentator.

Edward D. Haerrter, 1937. Principal of the high school from 1923 until his death in 1942, Haerrter is memorialized by a tablet in the school lobby that praises his devotion "to the training of youth as honest and useful citizens."

Center Playground, 1936. Now the site of Civic Square, the playground was developed after the town drained Durand's Pond and confined the Elizabeth River within a concrete flume built by the W.P.A. The high school is at left. At far left is the future site of the public library.

Lucille Manners, 1937. Known as Marie McClinchy when she attended high school here, Miss Manners was a popular vocalist who sang at the old Paper Mill Playhouse in Millburn.

Taking a Spin on the Ice at Center Playground, 1936. Star of radio and stage, Miss Manners returned to Irvington in February 1936 from performances at Radio City Music Hall to accept an award from Mayor Percy A. Miller which recognized "her grace, charm and talent." Afterward, she joined her fans for a spin on the ice.

American Legion Baseball, *c.* 1935. Sponsored by Irvington Post 16 and coached by "Doc" Gantz, American Legion baseball was the only organized ball played during the summer months. Tri-City Stadium at Mill Road and Union Avenue (where the bowling alley is today) was the home of semi-pro teams such as the Tuscan Farmers.

S.A.L. Drum & Bugle Corps, *c.* 1937. With over a hundred members, the Sons of the American Legion was popular with Irvington's youth. Charles F. Hausmann (1895–1973), standing at far right, directed the Drum & Bugle Corps during the Thirties. Most of the teen-agers pictured here on the high school's steps entered service after World War II broke out.

Clarence E. Chamberlain, 1930. He was principal of Frank H. Morrell High School from 1942 to 1950, when he retired after thirty-seven years in the Irvington school system.

Irvington Municipal Building, 1940. Designed by local architect Daniel A. Hopper Jr., the Colonial-style building began rising on the former site of Center Playground in late 1941. Built at a cost of $436,000, it was dedicated in May 1943, eighteen months after Pearl Harbor plunged the nation into war.

Seven
Kaleidoscopic Years

"Here We Go, Girls," 1940. Like a kaleidoscope, the Irvington of the Forties, Fifties, Sixties, and Seventies was constantly changing. When news came of the surprise Japanese attack of Pearl Harbor on December 7, 1941, it was as if the two decades since the armistice ending World War I had never been. Within days, America was again at war—and Irvingtonians were in the thick of it. When Bette Clemence, drum majorette, and cheer leaders (from left to right) Beverly Meander, Ruth Wade, Marjorie Meyers, Eleanor Kurfess, Ruth Kreter, and Nadeline Kellerhoff stepped on the field in the fall of 1940, 7,500 Irvington men had already registered for the draft.

Marlin Brinser and Bette Clemence, 1940. Brinser, who retired in 1964 after thirty-seven years at the high school, led the band to national prominence. The largest in the state during the Forties, it performed at the 1940 World's Fair.

Swiss Flag Swingers, September 1941. The high school band's half-time performances were so good that the band was the first from New Jersey to be invited to play at the old Polo Grounds during New York Giant's football game's half-time ceremonies.

Eleven Cheerleaders and One Cut-Up, 1942. Jerome Lewis (second from left, rear) graduated from Union Avenue School in 1940, and then spent two years at the high school where—if tradition is to be believed—he roller skated through the halls. Better known as Jerry Lewis today, he ushered at the old Rex Theatre on Chancellor Avenue and hung out at the Rex barbershop nearby.

Co-Ed Cooks, 1940. Seventh and eighth grade students at Chancellor Avenue School enjoyed Mrs. Sharp's cooking class. Pictured here are Alma Simonitsch, Herbert Ramo, Sally Baron, Adelaide Shortmeier, Lillian Reisinger, Martha Zufall, Ernest Hammer, Evelyn Friedland, Lorraine Lacy, Ruth Reilly, the Lemmerman cousins, and Jack Ginsberg.

Springfield Avenue at Lake Street, 1940. The squarish building on the corner had once been a Universalist church and roller skating rink, but now houses Joseph Walker's embroidery factory. Lake Street ran from Springfield Avenue to Durand's Pond, later Center Playground.

Springfield and Clinton, 1940. The Castle Theatre at far left was only one of several movie houses in town: the Rex on Chancellor Avenue, the Hindenburg on 18th Avenue, and the grandest of them all, the Sanford Theatre on Springfield Avenue opposite Sanford Avenue. When the Liberty near Lincoln Place opened, it featured vaudeville acts and a five-piece orchestra.

Springfield Avenue, Looking West, 1940. The buildings on both sides of the street were built by the Drake family in the Twenties. George W. Frost & Son, jewelers, came to town in 1895. Peoples National Bank, a few doors west of Frost's, was Irvington's third bank when it opened in 1926.

Union Avenue Looking West from the Center, 1940. Bibbo's has been an Irvington Center fixture for over fifty years. The Camptown Savings and Loan Assn. (now Investors Savings), founded in 1910, has been located on Union Avenue since 1924. Once known as the "the road to the Swamp Mills," Union Avenue took its present name after Union County was organized in 1857.

Springfield and Union Avenues, 1940. Drake's Feed Store gave way to this three-story office and retail building in the mid-Twenties. Nathaniel Drake built one of Irvington's finest homes in 1903 on the corner of Harrison Place and Clinton Avenue. Later, in 1927 it became the Haeberle & Barth Funeral Home.

Hindenburg Theatre, 16th Avenue, June 1940. Rumors that a tunnel connected the theatre, where German newsreels were shown, to Willy's Tavern across the street were no laughing matter to the merchants on 16th Avenue, many of whom would soon be driven out of business. The baker next door to the theatre offered a $500 reward "If anyone can prove we are Nazis."

Raising Funds for the Brits, 1941. On May 17, 1941, over a thousand people attended an entertainment and dance held at the Elks Club for British War Relief. The $1,118 raised was used to purchase an ambulance for the City of Liverpool. The committee, from left to right, are: (front row) Henry A. Schwedes, Leslie West, and Howard W. Baker; (rear row) Harry Knox, G. Archibald Day, and Frederic Stoddard.

The War on the Home Front, 1944. Salvage and scrap drives netted 15,000 pounds of table fat used for glycerine, more than 7,000 tons of metal (including a World War I howitzer that had stood on Camptown Common) and truckloads of paper. Here, air raid wardens meet at the Augusta Street School yard to celebrate their first 100 tons of scrap paper. Mayor Kruttschnitt stands third from left with Chief Air Raid Warden Ed Barrett to his left.

"Chic Uniforms Worn by Lionel Girls," 1943. At Lionel, production lines were converted to over one hundred different defense products. Irvington Varnish, Atlas Foundry, and Irvington Steel Works made components for a top-secret explosive device, later known as the A-bomb.

The Spirit of Webster Street, 1943. Thirty-eight families living on Webster Street sold over $1 million in war bonds to purchase two Flying Fortresses. Max Beinner, shown here with Mayor Kruttschnitt, spearheaded the effort. More than 7,000 Irvington men and women served during the war; 172 never returned home.

All for One, One for All, 1942. War or no war, it was politics as usual in Town Hall. Elected as a team in 1938, Commissioners (from left to right) Edward D. Balentine, J. Edward Jacobi, Herbert Kruttschnitt, Harry E. Stanley, and Percy A. Miller Jr. ran together again in 1942. In a surprise turn of events, Jacobi and Stanley were defeated by newcomers J. Elmer Hausmann and Edward J. McKenna.

Chancellor Avenue Playground, 1944. Viewed from the Chancellor Avenue bridge over the Elizabeth River, the playground occupies most of what once was Drake's Lower Pond. Union Avenue School, built in 1929, is seen in the distance, at center. Today Garden State Parkway traffic speeds through here.

Shrine of the Mother of Christ, 1944. Italian-Americans were drawn to Irvington when the Lionel Corporation moved here. By 1970 they were the town's second largest ethnic group. Anthony Zappulla, who built this shrine on Harper Avenue, led the annual Feast of the Assumption.

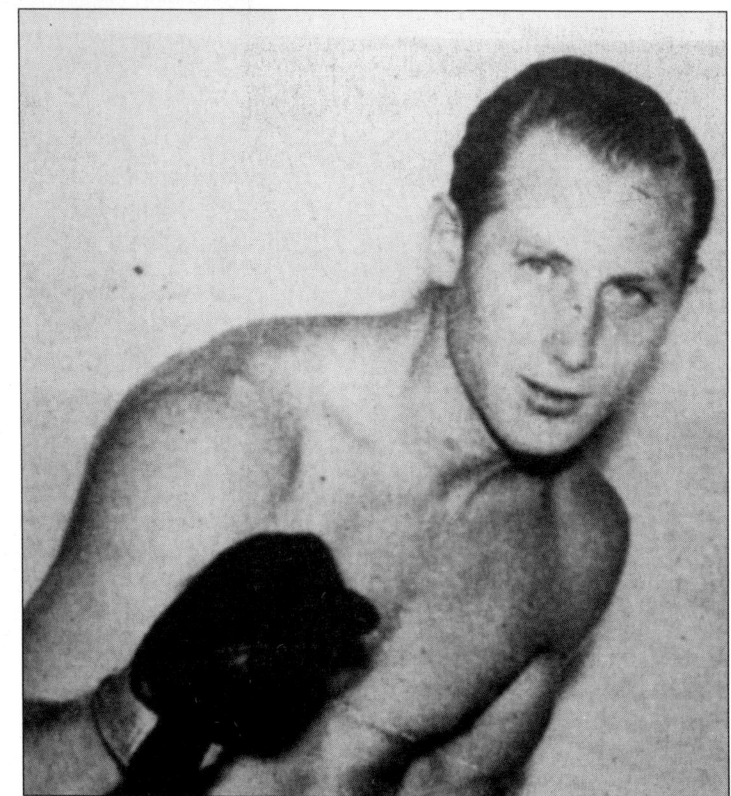

Charlie Fusari, *c*. 1945. Known as "The Milkman," he was a top welterweight contender in the Forties and early Fifties, taking on the likes of Sugar Ray Robinson and Rocky Graziano. When not in the ring, he delivered milk.

Baby Parade, Olympic Park. Two-year-old Nancy Faupel garners first prize as Snow White in the last Baby Parade at Olympic Park before the war began. Park attendance, in the doldrums during the Depression, broke new records during the war years as America's economy boomed.

On the Beach, c. 1950. During the Olympic Park pool's forty-three seasons, an estimated five million people paid admission. Sometimes the man-made sand beach was so crowded that there was barely enough room to spread a blanket. Built in 1923, the pool held 3.75 million gallons of fresh water.

The Roller Coaster and Motor Boats, 1964. Olympic Park closed after its final season in September 1965. An industrial park now occupies the site. The park's famous carousel, "Miss Liberty," was redesigned by Walt Disney artists, christened "Cinderella's Golden Carousel," and is now the centerpiece of a medieval courtyard in Fantasyland, Walt Disney World, Orlando.

Joe Basile, The Brass Band King (1889–1961). Affectionately nicknamed "Mr. Five by Five," the rotund bandleader was to entertain Olympic Park audiences for a record forty-nine years.

Rev. Harry Olson, 1945. One of Irvington's most popular ministers during the Forties, Olson was pastor of First Reformed Church from 1939 to 1952.

Grove Street School Kindergarten, 1951. Until 1900 Irvington was overwhelmingly Anglo-Saxon and Protestant. After the turn of the century, foreign-born and first and second generation Americans predominated, as the surnames in this class picture show. Mrs. Baddick's five- and six-year-old students included: Nan Mutnick, Barbara Poperak, Leslie Wilson, Emilio Suarez, Jeannie Mentus, Betty Jane Oleksik, Diane Siezer, Irene and Joan Schlosser, John Burns, Mark Resnick, and Aleda Jordan.

Rev. Msgr. Mieczyslaw Lankau, 1951. First pastor of Sacred Heart of Jesus Church on Grove Street, Rev. Lankau was buried in 1962 in front of the church he did so much to establish.

Laying the Cornerstone, 1950. Irvington's largest ethnic group in the Sixties and Seventies, the Poles settled in the Manhattan Park section along Grove Street after World War I. Featuring an altar of hand-carved Italian marble, Sacred Heart of Jesus Church took three years to build.

Rev. Eugene R. Gallagher. Founding pastor of St. Paul the Apostle R.C. Church, he celebrated the first parish Mass on June 20, 1948, at the Olympic Park Roller Skating Rink.

Opening Day, 1950. Both the sanctuary and school were dedicated in 1950. Here Rev. Gallagher welcomes the first students to the new school on Nesbit Terrace. Sister M. Richard of the Dominican Sisters of Caldwell was the first principal.

Oraton Parkway, 1950. Here's the view from the southeast corner of Springfield Avenue and Washington Street looking north toward Oraton Parkway. The Parkway Apartments (also known as the Marshall Street Apartments) are visible at the right. At far left is Dr. Albert Gaal's optometry office and the Moose Lodge next door.

Washington Avenue, *c.* 1950. Here's the opposite view, looking south on Washington Avenue to the Clinton Avenue and Ball Street intersection, a few years before the Garden State Parkway went through. Aberbach's Pharmacy was demolished when Ball Street was realigned. The row of old houses on Ball Street and Dr. Albion Christian's squarish home and office on Clinton Avenue were also lost to the Parkway.

Irvington Bus Terminal, 1953. Although the bus terminal remains much the same today, the First Christian Church to the right was demolished in 1953 when the Parkway was built. In the heyday of bus transportation, the terminal was a scene of busy activity as residents departed and returned from work in Newark, Hillside, Jersey City, and New York.

No Pushing, Please! Buses that stopped at the terminal included the # 90 Grove Street, which went as far as Bloomfield Avenue; the # 107 to New York City; the #94, which travelled along Stuyvesant Avenue from East Orange to Union; the #25 Springfield Avenue; the #13 Clinton Avenue; and the #5 and #6, two small independent lines that connected Irvington to Union, Hillside, and Elizabeth.

Chancellor Avenue at Chestnut Street, May 1948. Although under different ownership, the gas station, animal hospital, and used car lots are still there even today. A half-mile to the west, the Chancellor Avenue hill (from Hospital Hill to Union Avenue) was the site of soap-box derby elimination races during the 1930s.

Lyons Avenue between Union and Cleremont, *c.* 1950. All but three of the six- and eight-family walk-ups shown in this photo were demolished when the Garden State Parkway slashed through town in the mid-1950s. First called Route 4, the Parkway was originally proposed in 1944. Its final route along the Elizabeth River and Oraton Parkway prevented the loss of hundreds of houses and saved the town millions in tax ratables.

Oraton Parkway, 1951. Housing for returning World War II veterans lines Oraton Parkway in this view taken just a few years before excavation began here for the Garden State Parkway. The 1,744-unit Parkway Apartments at rear were built in 1951–52 on the old Ollemar tract at a cost of more than $12 million.

Construction of the Garden State Parkway Begins, 1955. A tunnel for the Elizabeth River is being constructed in this 1955 view looking north from Chancellor Avenue The four-story brick apartment house at far left is on Yale Avenue. The houses to the right face Cornell Street.

King and Queen of the Hallowe'en Parade, 1952. Commissioner (and later, mayor) Edward J. McKenna introduces the king and queen of the 1952 festivities in which 2,000 participated. A week later, Ike carried Irvington by 1,727 votes, and Jerry Lewis returned home to visit his old Union Avenue haunts.

Her Secret Boyfriend, 1957. Wende, the eight-year-old daughter of Carl and Wilma Perina, visits the Fall Flower Show held at the high school gymnasium. Until they were torn down in the early 1950s to make way for the First Congregational Christian Church, the 6,000-square-foot Jacobi greenhouses on the corner of Clinton Avenue and Civic Square were the last reminders of the town's long horticultural heritage.

Matthews Field, 1955. The athletic field behind Irvington High School was named in honor of William B. Matthews, the school's longtime football mentor. Two of his teams, the 1937 and 1944 squads, led the way with 8–1 records. The next best grid mark was Walter Marshall's 1959 squad.

The Winningest Coaches, *c.* 1955. Three of Irvington's winningest coaches pose in this candid snapshot: From left to right are: Milton "Mickey" Weiner, captain of the 1935 football team, assistant coach under Matthews, and high school principal; Bill Matthews, who retired in 1953 after thirty-two years coaching football; and Stanley G. Wnek, one of Irvington's stellar athletes, who succeeded "Doc" Gantz in 1954.

Stanley G. Wnek, 1963. Named varsity baseball coach in 1954, Wnek played with the Newark Bears and New York Yankees. He batted .545 in his senior year at Irvington High.

Civic Award Presentation, 1960. Christine McCloskey, at left, who served for twenty-five years as library director before her retirement in 1979, and George T. Hechtel, president of the Chamber of Commerce, relax after presenting the annual Civic Award to Verne Blake, at right, editor of the *Irvington Herald* for twenty-four years and an avid golfer.

Memorial Day, 1960. The Memorial Day parade and post-parade ceremonies at the monument on Camptown Common were a tradition for over fifty years. Unveiled in 1922, the bronze monument designed by Charles F. Keck depicts "a soldier, who, having dropped the implements of peace, has seized the weapons of warfare at the call of his country."

Frank H. Morrell High School, 1962. Erected at a cost of nearly $1 million, the high school was built largely through the unceasing efforts of Gustav Kruttschnitt, president of the Board of Education. Additions were built in 1955 and 1975. Principals have included Edward D. Haerrter, Clarence E. Chamberlain, Lloyd E. Taylor, Lester Rice, Alfred Bray, Milton Weiner, Philip Schectman, and William Mericle.

Toss of the Coin, 1962. Irvington "Tri" co-captains, Chippy Boehm, Bob Kuldanek, and Ken Oboz, await the toss of the coin before the game against Orange High School. According to Joe Carter Jr., *Herald* sports editor, Irvington High "maintained an outstanding position in New Jersey scholastic sports circles with its numerous standout teams and athletes, many of whom have achieved national recognition."

IHS Flag Swingers, 1963. Continuing the tradition started by Marlin Brinser, the flag swingers entertained football crowds at half-time. From left to right are: Carol Moran, Karen Weiner, and Karen Schreiner, who captained the 25-member team.

Class of 1964 Officers. The 660 students of the high school Class of 1964 were led by, from left to right: Janet Rone, secretary; Pat Gallagher, president; Barbara Pagano, vice president; and John Kozub, treasurer. Mrs. Evelyn Carlomusto and Mr. Robert Linnon, advisors, are smart enough to stand outside the booth.

Commission-Form of Government Defeated, 1962. Tired of nearly fifty years of political infighting and intrigue, Irvington voters discarded the commission-form of government in favor of the mayor-council form of government after a hard-fought campaign led by Mayor William Lovell (at left) and Change of Government Committee members, Dr. Charles I. Nadel (center), Michael A. Blasi (right center), and Irving Grossman (right).

Mayor Harry Stevenson, 1966–1974. Considered by many as one of Irvington's finest chief executives, ranking with Glorieux and Kruttschnitt, Stevenson stepped down in 1974 after twenty years of public service.

Irvington Day, September 1974. Irvington celebrated its centennial in 1974, capping the festivities with one of the largest parades ever seen in town. Here, the high school band passes the corner of Orange Avenue on its way to the Center. Earlier in the year, the Hoxie Brothers Circus came to town, recalling the days when Ringling Bros. Barnum & Bailey visited Ollemar field.

"And the Mayors Cut the Cake," 1974. A traditional cake-cutting ceremony followed in October at the Club Navaho Manor. From left to right are: Alan A. Siegel, centennial committee chairman; Mayor Stevenson; Joseph Galluzzi, Council president; Val Meissner, town clerk; Robert H. Miller, mayor from 1974 to 1982; Esther Schwartz, South Ward councilwoman; and Richard Hildebrand, tax collector. Meissner and Hildebrand were vice chairmen of the centennial committee.

Civic Square, 1974. This aerial shot looks southeast from a spot above the intersection of Clinton and Stuyvesant Avenues. On the far left is the the high school, then Clinton Avenue, the main library, the town hall, and the Public Safety Building (all fronting on Civic Square), and to the right is Springfield Avenue. Clinton and Springfield Avenues cross at the left of the picture. To the right, in the distance, is the senior housing on Union Avenue.

Irvington High School, 1974. The high school, with Matthews Field behind it, the public library and town hall, First Congregational Christian Church, and Orange Playground are all plainly visible in this aerial view taken from a vantage point above Springfield Avenue looking northeast toward the East Ward.

Irvington Center, 1974. From the Garden State Parkway looking west toward Civic Square, one sees the Irvington Bus Terminal, the Center itself with the Castle Theatre and Drake buildings, Krafte Camera, and Canadian Fur. Almost at the center of the photo is the burned-out remains of the Clinton Avenue School, ready for demolition.